John Thompson's Modern Course for the Piano

The SECOND GRADE BOOK

Something New Every Lesson

Stories and Biographical Sketches by
Laurence B. Ellert

Drawings by
Doris *and* George Hauman

Cover Illustration by
DiLonardo Design

Follows uninterruptedly and in progressive sequence the musical foundation developed by the "First Grade Book"

The Willis Music Company
Florence, Kentucky 41022-0548

PREFACE

Since the plan of the author's Modern Course for the Piano is to make the teachers' and pupils' work so pleasing that it will lead to the quickest and best results, THIS BOOK TAKES UP EXACTLY WHERE "THE FIRST GRADE BOOK" LEFT OFF. Briefly, it continues, uninterruptedly, to "make haste slowly", but surely and steadily.

With consideration for the needs of modern beginners, the contents of this, *The Second Grade Book*, are not limited strictly to piano music. In order that the young student may experience the joy of a course in appreciation as well as of pianism, examples (with explanatory notes) from light opera, ballet, grand opera, oratorio, songs, etc. have been included. Hence, the slogan "Something New Every Lesson" follows in logical sequence.

TECHNICAL AND MUSICAL PROGRESSION

In THE FIRST GRADE BOOK most of the examples remained necessarily in the five-finger position. In this book, the positions become gradually more extended. The thumbs are trained to pass under and the hands over; ledger lines are introduced; the pedals explained; major scales and their minors, both relative and parallel, are presented; examples in hand expansion, cadence chords, arpeggios, the dominant-seventh chord, as well as lessons in chord analysis, trill studies and, of course, the various touches are included. Most of the pieces are preceded by short technical exercises, which, in many cases, are subtle illustrations on how to practice—an art in itself.

MAKING MUSICIANS

Everything possible has been done to encourage the pupil to *think and feel musically*; to play with musical understanding so that his progress will be measured by increased enjoyment, as well as by increased technical proficiency.

Examples from the masters include works by Bach, Handel, Haydn, Mozart, Beethoven, Chopin, Liszt, Auber, Ponchielli, Bizet and Offenbach. It is the sincere wish of the author that students who complete this book will have become not only better pianists but also better musicians and that the urge to explore still deeper into the wonderful realm of music will have been intelligently stimulated.

John Thompson

P.S. Certificate of Merit (Diploma) will be found on page 91.

CONTENTS
"Something New Every Lesson"

Thumb UNDER the Second Finger (from *black* key)

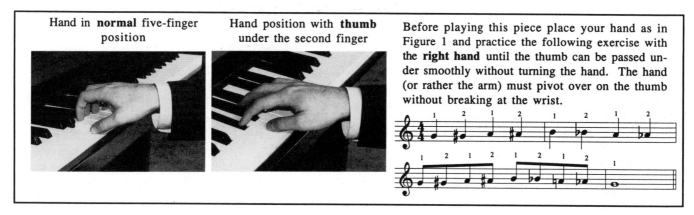

Hand in **normal** five-finger position

Hand position with **thumb** under the second finger

Before playing this piece place your hand as in Figure 1 and practice the following exercise with the **right hand** until the thumb can be passed under smoothly without turning the hand. The hand (or rather the arm) must pivot over on the thumb without breaking at the wrist.

In the Alps

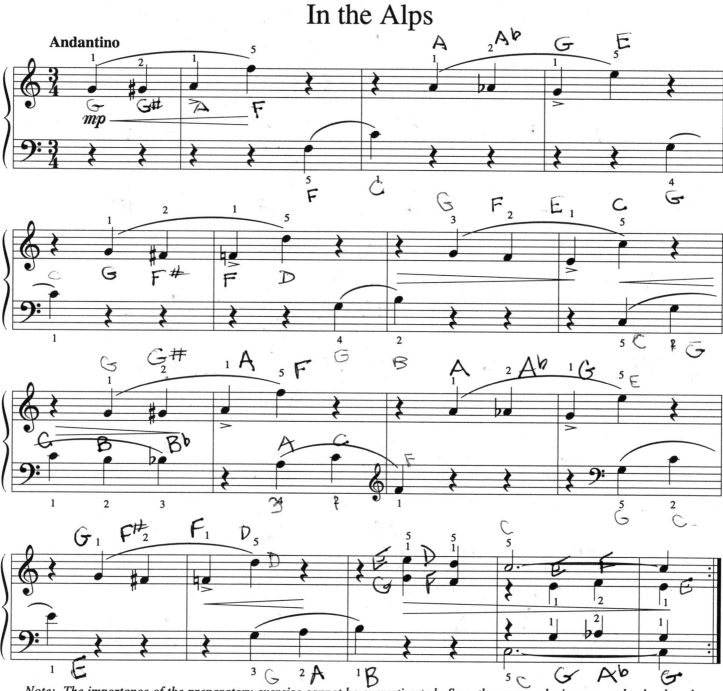

Note: The importance of the preparatory exercise cannot be overestimated. Smooth passage playing cannot be developed until the pivoting motion of the hand over the thumb has been mastered. These exercises should therefore be carried in review until they can be done with ease. For technical drills see page 89.

4

Light Opera or Musical Comedy is a play set to music in which part of the dialogue is sung and part of it spoken. In America, it usually has a happy ending. *Fra Diavolo* (Brother Devil) which derives its name from the hero, a famous Italian bandit, is a comic opera in 3 acts; music by the French composer, Daniel Francois Esprit Auber. It was first given in Paris in 1830 and in the United States in 1833.

Fra Diavolo as the Marquis ~ Act 1

Zerlina, an innkeeper's daughter is betrothed to Lorenzo, a soldier, but they are too poor to marry. Fra Diavolo, disguised as the Marquis San Marco, is travelling with two English tourists, Lord and Lady Allcash, in order to rob them of money and jewels. When the party arrives at the inn and tells of an attempted robbery by highwaymen, Zerlina, believing Fra Diavolo to be a real marquis, tells him the story of this bold bandit's life in the aria (solo) "On Yonder Rock Reclining". That night, after the guests retire, the marquis (Fra Diavolo) with several of his followers conceals himself in Zerlina's room to rob Lord Allcash. Lorenzo, who has been ordered to pursue the bandits, arrives with a party of soldiers and arrests two of the robbers while Fra Diavolo escapes to the mountains. In the third act, he is captured. Lorenzo receives a handsome reward, marries Zerlina, and they live happily ever afterwards.

Always
Be
Careful
to pass the thumb under smoothly

On Yonder Rock Reclining

D.F.E. Auber (1782-1871)

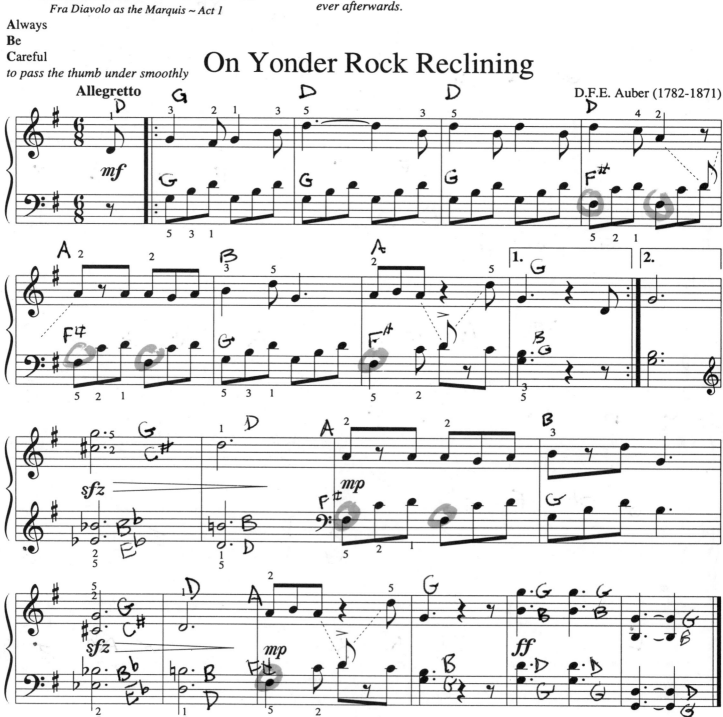

Hop O' My Thumb

For additional exercises see page 89.

Johann Sebastian Bach, one of the great masters of music, came from a musical family which for nearly 200 years had been noted among the townspeople of Eisenach, Germany. The story is told that his great-great-grandfather, a very jovial miller, sat in the door of his mill and sang and played his zither while the mill-wheel went 'round and 'round grinding the grain. When Johann was ten his father died and the young boy went to live with his brother, also a musician. As it was difficult to get music in those days, young Bach copied his brother's scores by moonlight. At the age of eighteen he would walk for miles, sometimes without food, to Hamburg, where he could listen to concerts. Toward the end of his life, Bach was a great favorite among the princes and kings. Nothing gave him more pleasure than having his many children and relations assemble in the Bach home and play music.

J.S. Bach

Menuet

J. S. Bach (1685-1750)

The Menuet is a very old dance of French origin. Its title is derived from the French word menu (small) and refers to the steps of the dance. It should be played at a rather deliberate tempo and as gracefully as possible. Be sure to observe all phrasing marks.

Ledger Lines

Ledger lines are short lines used on notes that lie ABOVE or BELOW the staff.

Ledger spaces are the spaces between the leger lines ABOVE or BELOW the staff.

Ledger lines or spaces are counted either UP or Down away from the staff and are very easy to recognize if we remember them as BORROWED LINES or SPACES.

Ledger Lines and Spaces ABOVE the Treble Staff

If we imagine five lines drawn above the TOP line of the treble staff and mark the leger lines, the FIRST BORROWED LINES will give us the position of A and B. TWO BORROWED LINES will show the position of C and D etc.

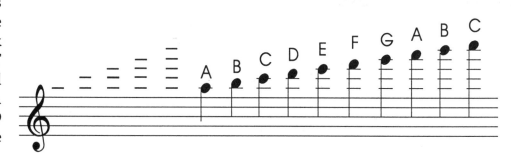

The following illustration shows how **all** ledger lines and spaces in the **bass clef** (above Middle C) are lines and spaces **borrowed** from the **treble clef.**

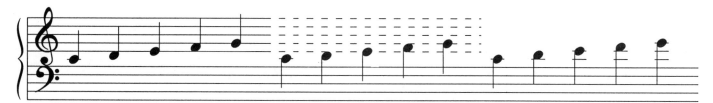

These notes in the **treble clef** when transposed to **bass clef** appear as above in music.

Note that the LINES indicated by the dotted extension of the staff show what LINES and SPACES were BORROWED from the TREBLE CLEF.

To read or write notes **below** middle C in the **treble clef** we **borrow** ledger lines and spaces from the **bass clef.**

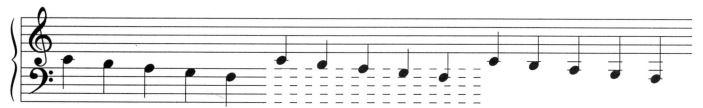

These notes in the **bass clef** when transpesed to **treble clef** appear as above in music.

Please notice that the notes whown on the dotted extension of the staff occupy the same LINES and SPACES BORROWED from the BASS CLEF.

8

Chromatic Progressions

This piece is built on chromatic progressions. Learn to play the *right hand melody pattern* first. Notice that it is repeated in several positions.

Right Hand Melody Pattern

Next, practice the following *left hand preparatory exercise.*

Left Hand

'Round The Village

Con moto

THE SIGNATURE FOR COMMON TIME

and its origin

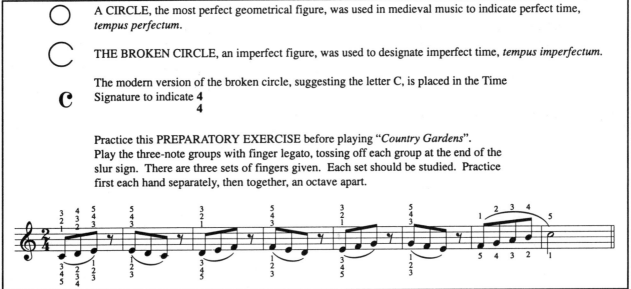

○ A CIRCLE, the most perfect geometrical figure, was used in medieval music to indicate perfect time, *tempus perfectum.*

C THE BROKEN CIRCLE, an imperfect figure, was used to designate imperfect time, *tempus imperfectum.*

𝄴 The modern version of the broken circle, suggesting the letter C, is placed in the Time Signature to indicate **4/4**

Practice this PREPARATORY EXERCISE before playing "*Country Gardens*".
Play the three-note groups with finger legato, tossing off each group at the end of the slur sign. There are three sets of fingers given. Each set should be studied. Practice first each hand separately, then together, an octave apart.

Country Gardens

Old English Morris Dance

From the *Morris Dance Tunes*, Set 1. By permission of Novello and Company, Limited.

BALLET is a pantomime telling a story in dance and music. The ballet is often introduced in an opera or stage piece aided by spectacular scenery and costumes. It is not necessarily part of an opera but may be complete in itself. "Dance of the

Hours" is a classic ballet which was written for the opera *La Gioconda* by Amilcare Ponchielli, an Italian composer, who was the teacher of Puccini. The opera was first performed in Milan, April, 1876, and in the United States in 1883.

The scene is Venice in the 17th century. La Gioconda, a beautiful street singer, is loved by Barnaba, a spy; but she spurns him because she is in love with Enzo, a Genoese nobleman. In revenge, Barnaba incites the people against Gioconda's blind mother, accusing her of witchcraft. The mother is saved by Enzo who, having incurred the displeasure of the "council," is obliged to disguise himself as a fisherman. In Act 3 , the great hall of the Ducal Palace is filled with masqueraders for the ball. The Duke announces the ballet in which the dancers, costumed as the Hours of Dawn, Day, Evening, and Night, portray the struggle between day and night. In the finale, the hours of light conquer the hours of darkness.

PHRASING: Ability to phrase gracefully is absolutely necessary to good piano playing. It not only adds style to your playing but also gives life and animation to the music.

Preparatory exercise

Dance of the Hours

Ponchielli (1834-1886)

Prelude

Christmas Carol

Some of the carols sung at Christmas time are older than folk-music. The word "carol," in the early centuries, meant *circle-dance*; a form in which the dancers sang to their own accompaniment. Carol dances were used for various festival seasons, New Year's Day, Easter, Christmas, etc. In medieval times, dances used by the nobility were called *Carolles*. This beautiful Christmas Carol from Hungary should be played joyously. Try to make it suggest sleigh bells and the cheerful spirit typical of the Yuletide. Play the left hand with *wrist staccato* and in the right hand be sure to make a distinction between the sustained chords and the staccato chords (wrist).

Cheerfully

The Pedals of the Piano

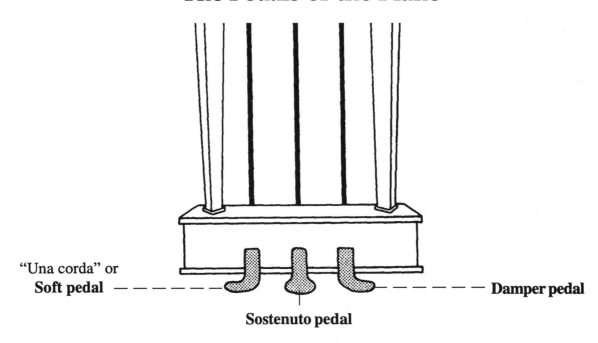

"Una corda" or
Soft pedal — **Damper pedal**

Sostenuto pedal

The modern grand piano is equipped with three pedals. The pedal on the right is called the **damper pedal** because when pressed down it raises up all dampers off the strings, thereby permitting all strings which have been struck to continue vibrating. In other words, it prolongs the TONE of strings affected.

The pedal on the left is known as the **soft pedal**. It gives a softer and lighter tone (although it functions differently on uprights than on grands). It is usually indicated in music by the words "una corda."

The middle pedal (on all grands) is called the **sostenuto pedal**. It sustains only the keys that are held down at the moment the pedal is applied. In many upright pianos the middle pedal is constructed so that it may be used as a **practice pedal**. When in use, a strip of felt is lowered between the hammers and the strings, thus deadening the sound and also the quality of tone.

For the present, we shall study the use of the **damper pedal** only. In the early part of the student's career it will be used for sustaining purposes, but later on it will be studied and used for color values as well.

There are many different signs to indicate when and where and how long to use the damper pedal, but in this book the following sign will be employed throughout:

Press down here   Release here

Play the following example, using only the third finger. Apply the **damper pedal** as indicated. LISTEN to the result!

(A)

Note how pleasant the sustained effect is to the ears! This is because *all of the notes are related* and form a chord.

Now play the next example,
fingering and pedaling as indicated.

(B)

This time the effect is blurred and very unpleasant because the notes are *not* related and form a series of dissonances annoying to the ear.

Play the following examples: **(C)** 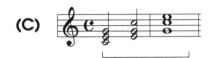   **(D)**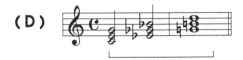

It is evident to the ear that example **C** is pleasant because only chords *of the same harmony* are sustained together.

Example **D** binds together, by use of the pedal, chords that are different harmonies, and the effect is a tonal jangle of harsh sounds.

It is quite obvious, therefore, that great care must be used in applying the pedal. Ones's playing can be enriched or marred by its use. Fortunately, at this stage of advancement it is simply necessary to follow the pedal markings strictly as indicated and correct results will follow.

THE SYNCOPATED PEDAL

The pedal should be applied *not* at the moment the keys are being pressed down, but *immediately afterward.* The reason for this will become clear after the student has advanced further along the road to pianism. For the present it is sufficient that the student form the habit of pedaling after the keys have been struck. This is sometimes called "syncopated pedaling." The following exercises will be found helpful.

EXAMPLE 1

Count: "ONE and TWO and THREE and FOUR and," etc.
Pedal *down* on the word "and;" pedal *up* on the numbers (1,2,3,4).

EXAMPLE 2

Count "ONE, TWO, THREE," etc.
Pedal *down* immediately *after* "ONE" in each measure.
Release pedal as you *say* "ONE" in each measure.

Teacher's Note: It is advisable to have students practice **left hand alone with the pedal** in all examples employing the pedal until its use becomes automatic and instinctive. This is particularly helpful because in the earlier grades the pedal is used mostly for the purpose of sustaining basses. Only the most elementary pedal effects should be attempted during the study of this book.

Distant Bells

L. Streabbog

To develop technical fluency use John Thompson's "First Studies in Style."

The Pedal With Arpeggio Groups

Use the pedal exactly as marked in the following example.

The arpeggio groups should be rolled rather than fingered and *tossed* from one hand to the other.

Follow the marks of expression and try to make a colorful sketch of this exercise from Duvernoy.

Etude

J.B. Duvernoy

Left Hand Alone

TEACHER'S NOTE: This short college song is presented purely as a recreation, and is not an essential part of the *Modern Course for the Piano*. From the pedagogic stand-point, its study will promote better left hand control, since the **left hand** is required to play both *melody and accompaniment*. Incidently, it offers an example for a pedal exercise.

Bill Grogan's Goat
(Humoresque for Left Hand alone)

College song

1. Bill Gro- gan's goat_____ was feel - ing fine,_____
2. The whis - tle blew,_____ the train drew nigh,_____

_____ Ate three red shirts_____ from off the line;
_____ Bill Gro - gan's goat_____ was doomed to die;

_____ Bill took a stick,_____ gave him a whack,_____
_____ He gave three groans_____ of aw - ful pain,_____

_____ And tied him to_____ the rail - road track.
_____ Coughed up the shirts_____ and flagged the train.

In the following piece the CHORDS should sound as though they were played on a church organ. This means that each chord must be as sustained as much as possible, that is, one chord must be connected to the next by means of the PEDAL.

NOTE THE NEW PEDAL MARK!

This sign is used to show that the PEDAL is released and pressed down again *immediately* in order to preserve an unbroken legato.   thus →

Sometimes you will see a pedal mark like this →

Or the word Ped. may be used like this → 𝄎. 𝄎. 𝄎. 𝄎.

Always remember that all three markings have the same meaning.

In Church

Andante, sostenuto e semplice

CARL CZERNY (*pronounced Chair'ne*) was born in Vienna, Feb. 21, 1791. His father, who was a music teacher, taught him to play the piano, and later he received instruction from Beethoven. When he was twenty-five, a European concert tour was planned for him, but there were so many disturbances because of war in Europe, that the public appearance was abandoned. He therefore decided to devote all of his time to teaching. His success was remarkable; among many noted artists to receive their training from him was the celebrated Franz Liszt, the greatest pianist that ever lived. As a composer, Czerny published over one thousand works, of which his many studies for the piano have been used steadily year after year.

Be careful to observe slurring the chord progressions.
Play the passages in 16th notes with a clean finger legato.

A Frolic in Velocity

C. Czerny (adapted)

For further development of finger legato use John Thompson's "The Hanon Studies."

The minstrel show was definitely an American form of entertainment. Minstrel companies were made up of a cast of men who blacked their faces, dressed in gaudy costumes, sang Negro songs, played banjos, danced taps, clogs, etc. Dan Emmett, the composer of "Dixie", was a member of the *Virginia Minstrels*. Stephen Foster wrote "Old Folks at Home" and some of his other famous songs for *Christy's Minstrels*. About 1870 , when minstrelsy was exceedingly popular, a Negro composer, James A. Bland, wrote this beautiful plantation melody which has been sung by the greatest artists in concert and over the radio.

Carry Me Back to Old Virginny

Introduction

James A. Bland

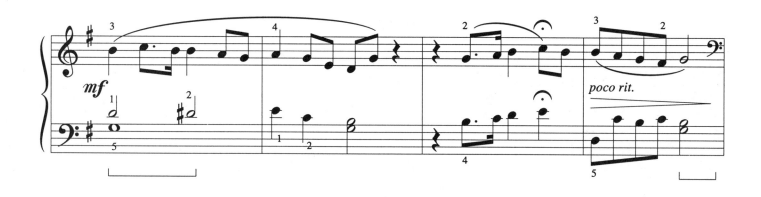

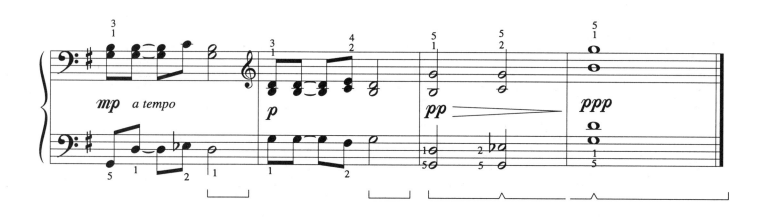

5770

Thumb *Under* the Third Finger

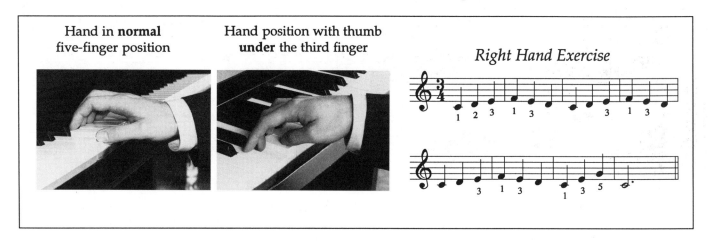

Hand in **normal** five-finger position

Hand position with thumb **under** the third finger

Right Hand Exercise

Reverie

Andantino

Note: See page 89 for supplementary exercises. Thoroughness in smooth passage playing is necessary.

Puck

Allegretto

Frédéric Francois Chopin was born in a village six miles from Warsaw, Poland. His father, a Frenchman who had come from Nancy, was a captain in the National Guard. He conducted a private school for the sons of the Polish nobility where Frédéric received his early education. His mother, for whom he entertained profound love, was pure Polish. She encouraged him at an early age to study music and he advanced so rapidly that, at the age of nine years, he played a concerto at a public concert. After the concert he seems to have been more concerned about his new collar than the effect his brilliant playing made on the audience, for he remarked to his mother: "Everybody was looking at my collar."

In 1831, Chopin went to Paris to make his home. It was there, in the drawing-rooms of the French aristocracy, that he fascinated his hearers with that wonderful playing which earned for him the name, *The Poet of the Piano*. He was never of robust health and during the last years of his life his frail body broke under the strains of his concerts, teaching and social activities. He died in Paris at the age of 39.

Prelude in A Major

Chopin (1810-1849)

SCALES IN EXTENDED FORM

Thorough familiarity with scales means better keyboard technic

SCALES should now be practiced in extended form - that is, NOT DIVIDED BETWEEN THE HANDS.
Continue with the preparatory exercise on page 89 until the hands can be passed over smoothly.

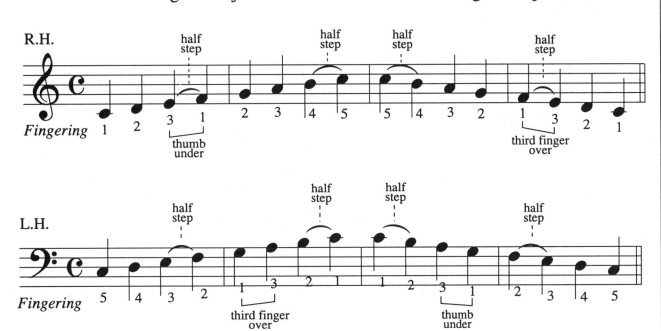

Ascending C major scale   Descending C major scale

Rules and Guides for the fingering of all the scales are shown on the charts, page 86. New scales should be studied at the direction of the teacher.

When the scale in extended form has been mastered by each hand separately, it is advisable to practice the hands together *first in contrary motion*, since this causes the *same fingers* to be used simultaneously in both hands. Later, they may be studied in parallel motion.

C MAJOR SCALE IN CONTRARY MOTION

C MAJOR SCALE IN PARALLEL MOTION

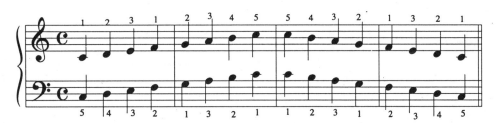

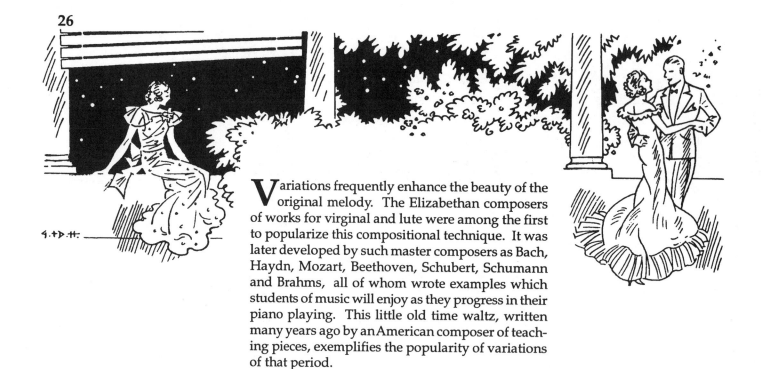

Variations frequently enhance the beauty of the original melody. The Elizabethan composers of works for virginal and lute were among the first to popularize this compositional technique. It was later developed by such master composers as Bach, Haydn, Mozart, Beethoven, Schubert, Schumann and Brahms, all of whom wrote examples which students of music will enjoy as they progress in their piano playing. This little old time waltz, written many years ago by an American composer of teaching pieces, exemplifies the popularity of variations of that period.

Starlight Waltz

Tempo di Valse

C.S. Brainard

Fine

Set a good tempo and keep it intact.

A waltz in 3/8 time is played considerably faster than one in 3/4.

Note the accent on the second beat which occurs very frequently.

The last Variation may require separate practice for the right hand. The groups in 16ths should be cleanly fingered and rolled off at the end of each phrased group.

Pedal only where marked.

TEACHING THE MINOR SCALES

There are two distinct approaches to teaching the MINOR SCALES; (1) the RELATIVE minor; (2) the PARALLEL minor. Although each method has decided merit, teachers differ in the choice of approach. For that reason both methods have been presented in the following pages and either may be used according to preference.

WHY DIFFERENT METHODS ARE USED

Teachers who use the RELATIVE minor approach do so because the key signature remains the same for both major and minor.

The PARALLEL minor approach is used because it causes less complication in the matter of fingering, especially in the WHITE KEY MINORS where the *fingering remains exactly the same* as in the PARALLEL MAJORS. However, the pupil should finally know BOTH approaches. For instance, after having played G major, the student should be able at once to play either G minor or E minor with equal facility. A debate, therefore, on the merits of either approach is rather useless.

HARMONIC MINOR FIRST

In the opinion of the author it seems unwise to attempt teaching all three forms of the minor (to the average pupil) at once. An old rule: "One thing at a time," is quite applicable to minor scales. Experience proves that if the Harmonic form is learned first in *all keys*, the result is one of less confusion and more perfect mastery, both analytical and technical, on the part of the student. Afterwards, when the scales are being reviewed for the second time, the other forms of the minor may be taught, thus showing the evolution of the minor scale from NATURAL to MELODIC to HARMONIC.

See chart on pages 86 and 87.

FORMING MINOR SCALES
The Relative Minor Approach

Every major scale has a *Relative Minor* scale.

The Relative Minor scale begins on the sixth degree of the Major scale.

There are three forms of the minor scale, namely NATURAL minor, MELODIC minor and HARMONIC minor. For the present we shall consider only the HARMONIC minor.

The Harmonic Minor is formed from the (Relative) Major Scale by raising the Seventh note (of the minor scale) one half step.

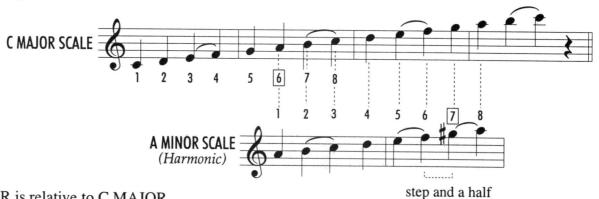

A MINOR is relative to C MAJOR.

The fingering for A minor is the same as that for A major.

Observe that the minor scale employs the same notes as the (Relative) major scale, except the seventh, which is raised ONE HALF-STEP.

A minor key has the *same signature* as the Relative Major Key.

NOTE TO TEACHERS: Teachers who prefer to teach all three forms of the minor scale at this point should use the chart on pages 86 and 87.

FORMING MINOR SCALES
The Parallel Minor Approach

Every major scale has a *Parallel Minor* scale.

The Parallel Minor scale begins on the *same note* as the Major scale.

There are three forms of the minor scale, namely NATURAL minor, MELODIC minor and HARMONIC minor.

For the present we shall consider only the HARMONIC minor.

The Harmonic Minor is formed from the (Parallel) Major Scale by *lowering the Third and Sixth degrees one half-step.*

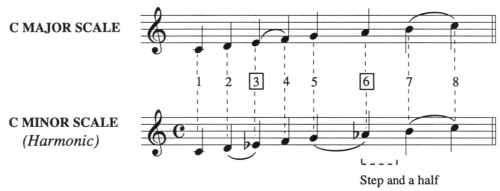

C MINOR is *parallel* to C MAJOR.

The fingering remains the same as in the major scale.

Observe that the lowered notes always occur at the point where the *third fingers play together.* (This rule will hold good for the first five WHITE KEY minor scales, i.e. C, G, D, A, E.)

MAJOR AND MINOR MODES

Note that the First Theme of this piece is in the key of C major and that the Second Theme is in the key of A minor, relative to C major. This is but another illustration of the *Law of Contrast*~the first law of all Art.

A Journey in the Arctic

Suggestions for Supplementary Material~ use John Thompson's "First Studies in Style."

First Theme

Coda

4th Finger CROSSING THUMB

The Sky Pilot

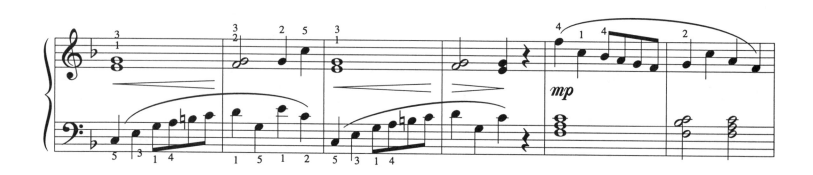

Preparatory Exercise

Hide and Seek

See page 87 for origin of melodic minor scale.

A study in smooth **finger legato**

Allegro

Old French Melody

It is frequently claimed that the national music of Hungary is really the music of the Hungarian gypsies. At any rate, the Hungarian composer, Franz Liszt, wove the gypsy music of native folk tunes into fifteen Hungarian Rhapsodies. This type of music is characterized by abrupt changes in mood and rhythm and, therefore, has tonal effects all its own. In the following example, be sure to play each theme with marked contrast. The opening theme should be played in a slow tempo and melancholy mood and the fiery second theme should be alive with animation and dash.

The Gypsy Camp

Very slowly (sad and melancholy)

Suggestions for supplementary material: John Thompson's **The Hanon Studies**

Very fast (with fire and dash)

Presto

G*rand Opera* is a play set to music in which the characters act and sing their thoughts instead of speaking them. *Don Giovanni* (Don Juan) was written by the great Austrian composer, Wolfgang Amadeus Mozart. The libretto by Lorenzo da Ponte is based on the story *The Stone Guest*. This great opera was produced for the first time in Prague in 1787 and received its United States premiere in 1826. There are two acts and the plot is laid in Seville during the Seventeenth Century.

Don Juan, a roguish Spanish nobleman, and his mischievous servant, Leporello, are always making people unhappy. Don tries to press his attentions on Anna. Her father, the Commandant, unexpectedly arrives. They fight a duel. The Commandant is killed, and Don Juan and his servant escape. The townspeople erect a statue in honor of their dead Commandant. While fleeing along a deserted road, Don Juan meets an old sweetheart, Elvira, who reproaches him but he escapes, leaving her alone with Leporello. We now find the cavalier in his palace flattering a beautiful peasant girl, Zerlina. He orders a gala festival and we hear the strains of the "MINUET", that graceful and courtly dance of the incomparable Mozart. Don Juan attempts to run away with Zerlina but is prevented by the appearance of Anna, in search of the murderer of her father, and Elvira, who seeks revenge; Don Juan again takes to his heels. That night, near the statue of the slain commandant, Don and his servant plan other schemes. Suddenly, the statue speaks, warning them to mend their ways. Flippantly, Don invites the statue to dine with them. During the banquet, a heavy tramping is heard on the stairs. The statue enters the room, Don Juan seizes the marble hand and instantly the floor opens and demons drag the wicked Don Juan down amid flames and lightning.

Minuet from "Don Giovanni"

Mozart (1756-1791)

The MAZURKA is a lively round dance and one of the national dances of Poland. Remember that in all dance forms, rhythm is of paramount importance. Keep a steady, even tempo and observe all ACCENTS.
This piece is in the key of A MINOR – relative minor to C major.

A Little Polish Dance

Mazurka

ETUDE

Allegro

Adapted from Kohler

A little line over a note, means *SOSTENUTO*, (well sustained). Give to these notes your best singing quality of tone.

In the following example play the scale passages with smooth finger legato and try for as much contrast as possible between *legato*, *staccato* and *sostenuto*.

Always
Be
Careful
to keep wrist relaxed

The Hare and the Hounds

Allegro

Fine

D.C. al Fine

Additional scale exercises will be found on page 90.

Try to play "Off We Go" as gracefully as possible.
Preserve an even finger legato and toss off the end of each phrase, indicated by the curved line.

PREPARATORY EXERCISE

The following exercise should be practiced daily until the chords lie comfortably under the fingers and until the change can be made without effort.

Off We Go!

Allegro grazioso

Streabbog

Chromatic scale

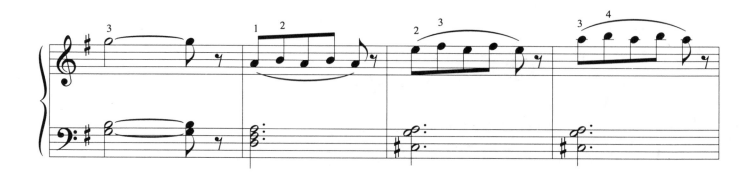

Up-arm stroke and arm impulse

This tune is quite characteristic of the gypsy life in the old days of Russia. It has all of the rhythmic features and the spirit of the furious dances so typical of the Russian peasants.

It should be played with a free, fiery abandon employing sharp accents and sharp staccato. The accented chords, coming as they do at the end of a short phrase, should be played with decided UP-ARM strokes. Be sure to play the repeated chords that follow with one-arm impulse. Use pedal sparingly.

Two Preparatory Exercises

No. 1. for the Right Hand

No. 2. for the Left Hand

Dark Eyes
Russian Gypsy Dance

Folk Song

CADENCE CHORDS

What a *period* is to a sentence, a *cadence* is to music. In other words, a *CADENCE* is the *end of a musical sentence.*

The principal **TRIADS** of the scale are those found on the **FIRST, FOURTH** and **FIFTH** degrees. They are important because they are the *chords used in forming CADENCES.*

These chords are named **TONIC, SUB-DOMINANT** and **DOMINANT** as shown below.

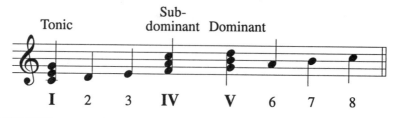

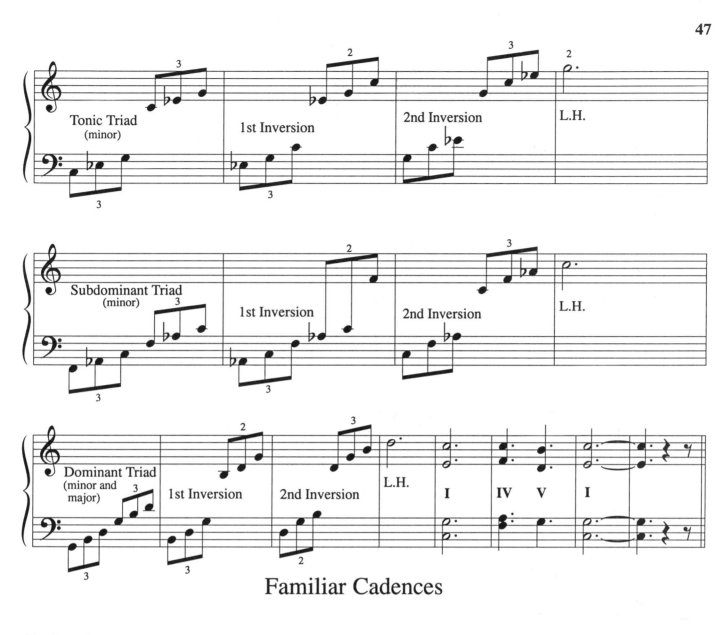

Familiar Cadences

Tonic and Dominant Chords

Tonic and Subdominant Chords

Tonic, Dominant and Subdominant Chords

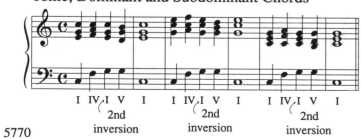

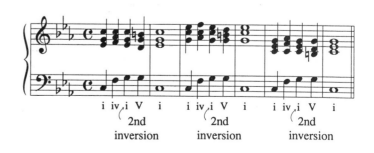

Here is a study in CHORD ANALYSIS.

Write the *name* and *inversion* of each chord in the following example. When you can play the Preparatory Exercise, follow with the Etude showing the chords in broken form.

Preparatory Exercise

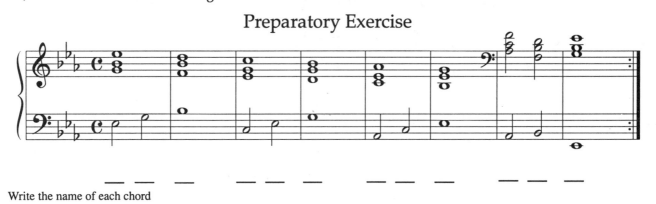

Write the name of each chord

Étude

Moderato

L.H.
over

     For further development of the rolling attack use John Thompson's "The Hanon Studies."

You have learned that TRIADS on the 1st, 4th and 5th degrees of the scale~ TONIC, SUB-DOMINANT and DOMINANT~ are called CADENCE CHORDS.

The TRIAD on the 5th degree, the DOMINANT, often appears with the addition of a minor 7th~ (1,3,5,7) and is known as the CHORD OF THE DOMINANT SEVENTH.

Chord of the Dominant-Seventh

The minor seventh is a pleasing dissonance and adds a feeling of motion to the chord, since all dissonances are active in character and must move to a consonant interval before a feeling of rest is secured.

BECAUSE THE CHORD CONTAINS FOUR NOTES, THREE INVERSIONS ARE POSSIBLE

Dominant 7th Chord
and
THREE INVERSIONS

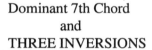

Root position *1st Inversion* *2nd Inversion* *3rd Inversion*

Root position *First Inversion* *Second Inversion* *Third Inversion*

CADENCE CHORDS USING THE DOMINANT-SEVENTH CHORD

Play the following cadences and note the feeling of activity given the dominant chord by reason of the added minor seventh.

I V^7 I   I V^7 I   I V^7 I

THE DOMINANT-SEVENTH IN ARPEGGIO FORM

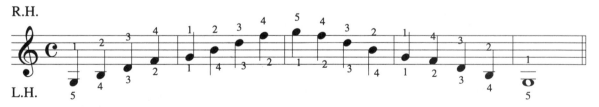

Examine the pieces studied thus far in this book and see how many *Dominant-Seventh Chords* you can locate.

Ludwig van Beethoven, one of the greatest of musicians, was born Dec. 16, 1770, in Bonn-on-the-Rhine, Germany. His father, a tenor singer in the village choir, was cruel and sometimes beat the boy when he did not practice. His mother was kind and patient. Her death, when he was seventeen years old, brought him sorrow which he never seemed to forget. When still a boy, he was made assistant organist in the cathedral, a position which he held until 1792. He also played second viola in the theatre orchestra. One day when he was on a visit to Vienna, he met Mozart who was so impressed with Beethoven's playing that he exclaimed: "He will give the world something worth listening to."

Beethoven loved to compose his music while wandering through the cool forest and listening to the voices of nature. At the age of thirty he began to grow deaf; in later years he was unable to hear his own compositions.

Romanze
From 5th Sonatina

Beethoven (1770-1827)

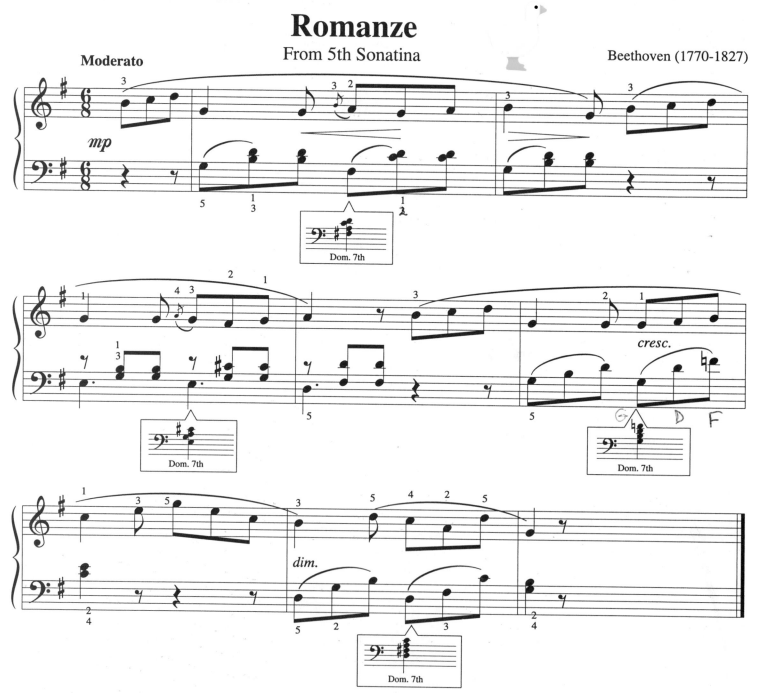

A Grace Note is a little note used as an ornament. It has no time value and should be "flicked" into the principal note which follows as quickly as possible. It is always shown as a small note with a slanting line drawn through its stem, thus ♪.

ALLA BREVE

When the TIME SIGNATURE shows a line drawn through the broken circle thus, ₵ , it is called *Alla Breve* time and it indicates *two counts to the measure*, with *one count to each half-note*.

Learn the following example first in four-four TIME, i.e., four counts to the measure and one count to each quarter-note. When it has been perfectly mastered, increase the *tempo*, counting but *two to the measure* and *one to each half-note*.

Scherzino

See glossary on page 88 for the meaning of Scherzino.

Franz Liszt, born in Raiding, Hungary, was a very delicate and sickly boy until he reached the age of six. Then, one day, while his father was playing a concerto on the piano, little Franz came up beside him and implored him to repeat the last movement over and over again. "What would you like to be when you grow up?" asked his father lighting his pipe. "That man there!" said the boy pointing to a picture of Beethoven. The next day his father began to give him lessons. Franz spent hours practicing the scales and made such rapid progress that he played in a concert by the time he was nine years old. The performance was so brilliant that everybody wanted to meet him and six of the nobles present raised funds to send him to Vienna for study with Czerny.

Later "little Liszt" enjoyed a greater triumph, for, when Beethoven heard him play, he was so amazed by Franz's wonderful technique that he went to the stage, grasped the child, and kissed him on the forehead.

Because the little village of Raiding was rather isolated, it became a camping place for wandering gypsies, who, as they arrived in their wagons, would pitch their tents in the square. At night, amid the blaze of great bon-fires, the men with violins and cymbals, and the girls in brilliant colored dresses, earrings, and necklaces, would dance and sing the rugged folk-tunes of Romany. Little Franz would drink in these weirdly abrupt rhythms and melodies which later became so evident in his famous *Hungarian Rhapsodies*.

Theme from Liebesträume No.3

A Dream of Love

ere is an example of sudden and abrupt contrast in mood, typical of Slavonic music. Note that the first theme is played very slowly and in lyric style - which is to say, in the manner of a song. It is rather pensive in character. But at the double bar it suddenly bursts into a very excitable dance, played *Allegro*. The dancers whirl about, gathering more and more impetus until the measure marked *molto rit.*-(much ritard) is reached. Here in one measure the tempo slows down to that of the opening theme and the piece ends on the lament with which it began.

Preparatory Exercises

A Little Slavonic Rhapsody

Andante

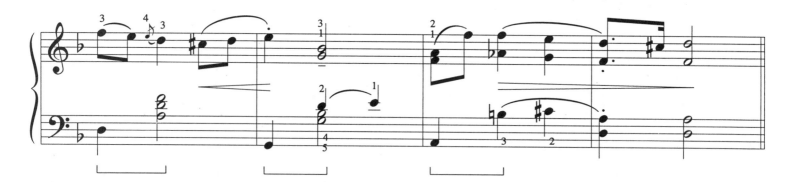

Allegro con brio

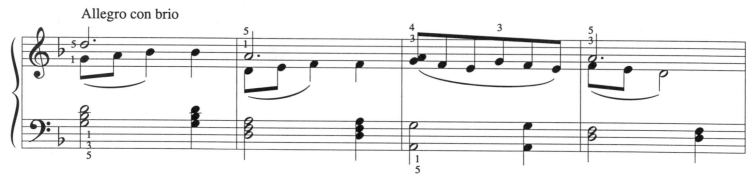

Tempo I

dim. e molto rit.

Oratorio derives its name from the oratory *(a chapel in a church)* in which a monk, Fillipo Neri, used to deliver his sermons on Biblical history during the Sixteenth Century. These discourses were illustrated by sacred songs. The modern oratorio consists of solos, duets, broad majestic choruses and recitatives with full orchestral accompaniment. It is distinguished from opera by the absence of action, costumes, and scenery. Usually the story is based on some text from the Bible. In the Eighteenth Century, Bach, Handel and Haydn developed the oratorio to its highest standard.

Messiah was written by George Frideric Handel, a German composer who spent many years in England and who lies buried in Westminster Abbey. The story concerns the prophecies and coming of Jesus. It is said that Handel wrote this long oratorio in twenty-four days. When a great choir sang the Hallelujah *Chorus* at a performance of the *Messiah* in London, King George II and his nobles rose to their feet to show their reverence for this great music. The entire audience stood up with him and to this day it is customary for an audience to stand during the singing of this chorus.

Hallelujah Chorus

Handel (1685-1759)

Etude

Roll the left hand groups

Skipping Through The Forest

Suggestions for supplementary material~use John Thompson's "First Studies in Style."

ARPEGGIOS
(Broken Chords)

A broken chord is called an *Arpeggio.*

Arpeggio is an Italian word meaning "in the style of a harp".

Arpeggios exist in many forms, but small hands should be restricted to arpeggios in closed form - that is, chords that remain in the octave position - until sufficient stretch has been developed to encompass the crossing called for in extended arpeggios, smoothly and easily.

The following forms will be found to be very beneficial and will afford interesting practice.

RULE FOR FINGERING: 1st, 2nd, and 5th fingers are always used by both hands in all positions. The use of the 3rd or 4th finger is governed by the stretch involved. If there is *only one white key* between the note played by the 5th finger and the next note of the chord, *use the fourth finger.*
When there are *two white keys* lying between, *use the third finger.*

Practice with well-articulated finger legato.

This form should be practiced with the Rolling Attack and sharply tossed off.

Practice in various keys as directed by the Teacher.

Étude

Scherzando

H. Berens

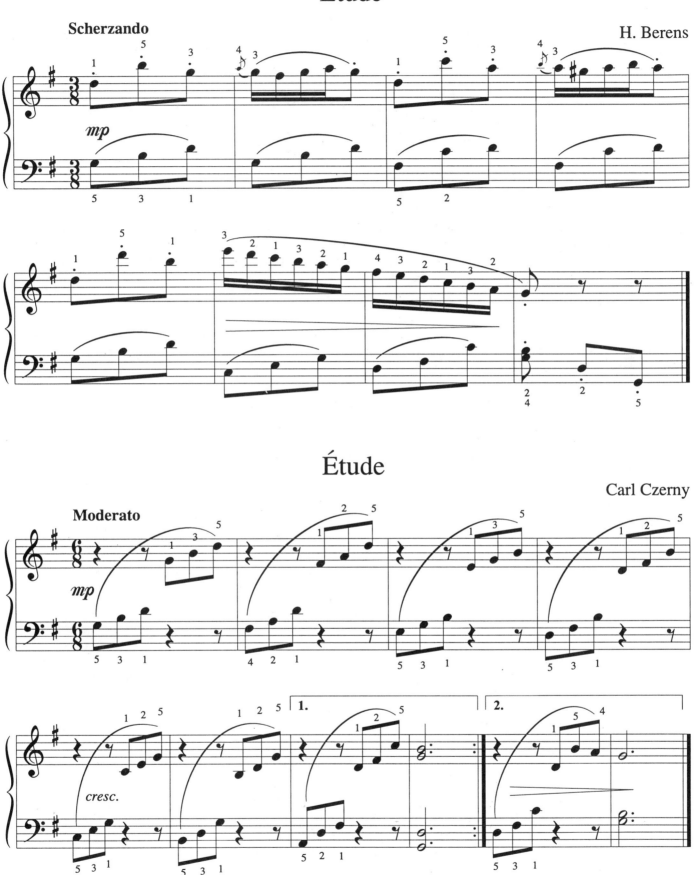

Étude

Carl Czerny

Moderato

60

Preparatory Exercise

When playing this exercise roll the ARPEGGIOS from one hand to the other, and try to play them so smoothly and evenly that the passages will sound as though they were *played with ONE hand*.

Hinkey, Dinkey, "Parley Voo"

Arpeggio Variations

The doughboy he went over the top
Because he had no place to stop,
From gay Paree he heard guns roar
And all he learned was "je t'adore."

World War I Song

5770

Deep River

The songs sung by the slaves on the plantations, at prayer meetings, baptisms, and on the levees are often referred to as Spirituals, and are part of our American tradition. The music is full of rare and sorrowful melodies which are as rich, colorful, and warm as any folktune. The Bohemian composer, Dvořák, used some of these tunes in his symphony, *From the New World*.

Andante espressivo

Plantation Hymn

Moths

Scherzino

TRIPLET is the name given to a group of THREE notes that are intended to be played in the time ordinarily given to TWO notes of equal value.

For instance:- THREE eighth notes played in the time of TWO eighth notes,

THREE quarter notes played in the time of TWO quarter notes and so on.

In the following example there are triplets applied to scale figures.

Play this example with clean, articulated finger legato. It is fine practice for developing evenness of touch.

Grandpapa Jonathan
Diatonic figures in Triplets

For additional exercises in articulated finger legato use John Thompson's "The Hanon Studies."

Georges Bizet was born in Paris, October 25, 1838. His mother taught him the rudiments of music when he was only four years of age and he was sent to the Conservatory before he was nine. He won the *Grand Prix de Rome* when he was nineteen and while studying in Italy he submitted, instead of the prescribed mass, an opera which was highly praised. He was a remarkably fine pianist although he did not perform in public. His fame and renown rest upon his two *L'Arlesienne Suites* and the opera, *Carmen*, which placed him in the front rank of modern French composers. The example following is from the first act of *Carmen* and shows the scene wherein Carmen sings and dances in her attempt to captivate Don Jose, a Spanish captain of the guard. A Habanera is a Spanish song and dance which really dates back to Africa by way of Cuba. It was imported into Cuba by Negro slaves and afterwards it naturally found its way into Spain. As in all dance forms rhythm is uppermost. Note the *alla breve* TIME- which means two counts to the measure and one count to each half-note. Learn it first, however, in four-four time. Let the staccato be sharp and brittle and do not overlook the two-note slur in each measure.

Habanera from "Carmen"

Bizet (1838-1875)

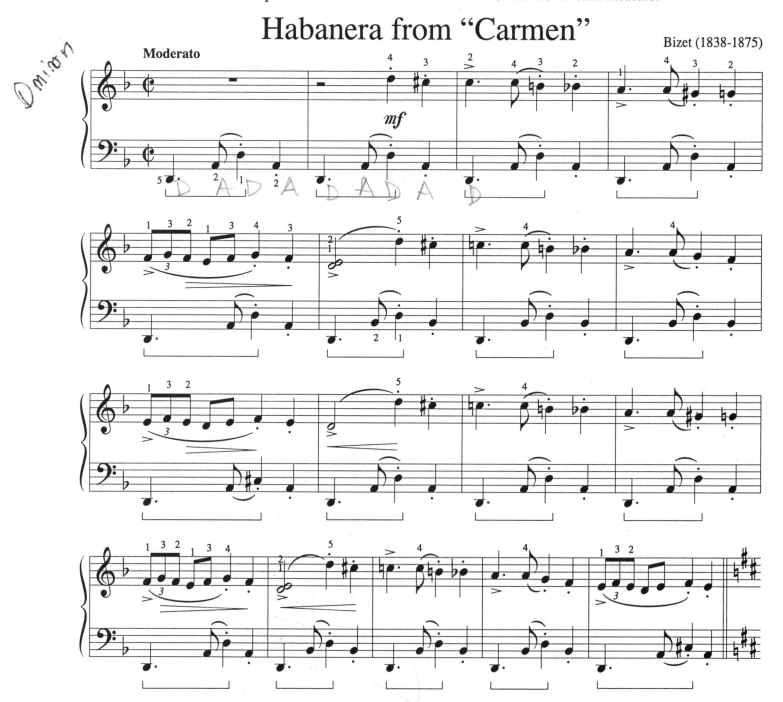

The Bee and the Clover

Adam Geibel

By Permission of The Boston Music Co. owners of the copyright.

Broken Chords in Triplets

A Trial Flight

THE TRILL

The TRILL is an ornamental figure which is very effective when well performed. It consists of an alternating shake between the principal note (the note written) and the next note above. The early keyboard instruments had very little sustaining qualities and the Trill was used originally to give the effect of a long, sustained tone. The number of notes played in a Trill is entirely optional with the performer.

This is the sign of the Trill, *tr*

Play the trill figures in the following example with close finger action. The fingers should actually "ride" the keys.

Preparatory Practice

The Nightingale and the Cuckoo

Two Guitars

Russian Gypsy Song

PREPARATORY EXERCISE

Learn to trill the first in 8th notes like this.

No. 1

etc.

Later in 16ths like this.

No. 2

The waved line (﹏) after *tr* indicates the duration of the TRILL.

Song of the Birds

Moderato

Jacques Offenbach was born in Cologne, Germany but at an early age settled in Paris and became a naturalized Frenchman. At the age of fourteen he joined the orchestra of the Opera Comique as a cellist. He originated a rather individual style of comic opera known as *opéra bouffe*, many of which, together with his ballet pantomime, were produced in his own theater, the Bouffes-Parisiens. His greatest work, the *Tales of Hoffmann*, was produced after his death. The first performance was given in Paris, Feb. 10, 1881 and in the United States in 1882.

The poet Hoffmann and his student friends of Nuremburg are making merry in the tavern while he tells of his three unhappy love adventures. The scene changes, Hoffmann is given a pair of magic glasses through which he sees Olympia, his first love, who is in reality a beautiful mechanical doll. He pleads to dance with her and they waltz so madly and rapidly that Hoffmann falls in a swoon. The glasses break and he learns that his love was an illusion. In the next act (in Venice), he discovers his friend, Niklaus, with a captivating lady, Giulietta, seated in a gondola, singing the "Barcarolle" in the mystic moonlight. He falls in love with her, fights a duel with his rival, and kills him, but, to the bitter disappointment of Hoffmann, Giulietta elopes with another. He then goes to Munich and wins the heart of the lovely Antonia, a delicate singer with a wonderful voice, whose doctor warns her that if she sings she will bring on a fatal illness. The wedding of Hoffmann and Antonia is set for the next day. In her happiness she sings and falls lifeless in her father's arms. The "Tales" are ended, the students depart and Hoffmann, sad and lonely, is consoled by the Muse of Poetry.

> **Play with a swinging six-eight rhythm to suggest a swaying gondola drifting under moonlight, a night in Venice.**

Barcarolle from "Tales of Hoffmann"

Offenbach (1819-1880)

Franz Joseph Haydn

Franz **Joseph Haydn** was born in Rohrau, Austria, in 1732. His genius attracted attention when he was very young and he is often called the father of instrumental music. In his early thirties he enjoyed the patronage and friendship of the wealthy Prince Esterhazy and consequently spent much time in Hungary. While there, he developed a keen interest in the music of the Hungarian gypsies. The composition below is an air from the last movement of Haydn's trio for piano, violin and 'cello, very properly called the "Gypsy Rondo". This music is characteristic of the Gypsy folk, full of light heartedness and the joy of living. All of Haydn's work is characterized by simplicity, perfect finish, the avoidance of meaningless phrases, and firmness of design. Use clearly articulated finger legato in the right hand in playing the "Gypsy Rondo" and do not overlook the occasional staccato notes.

Theme from Gypsy Rondo

Haydn (1732-1809)

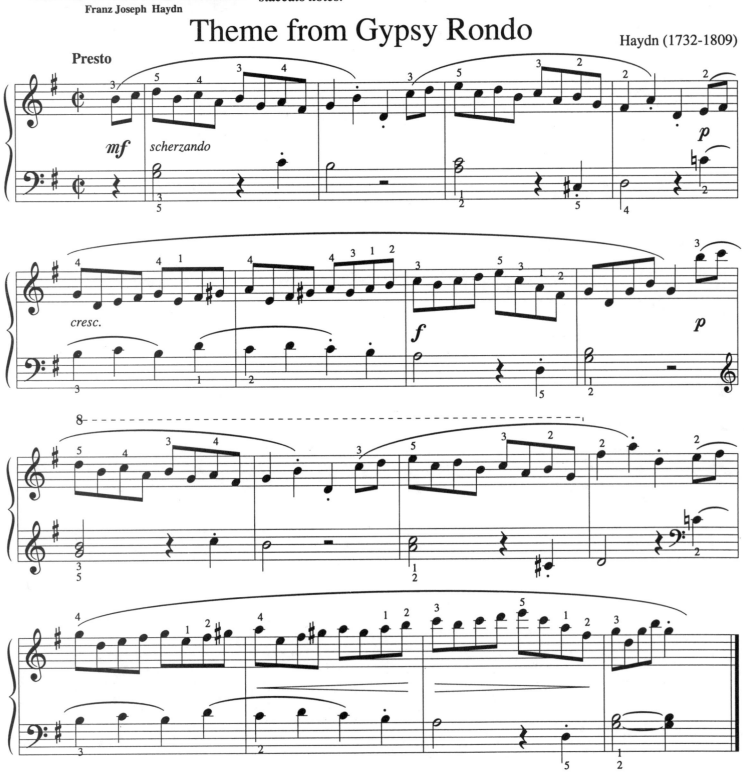

ROTARY (or Rolling) ATTACK

In the following examples, the groups in 16th notes should be rolled rather than fingered. Keep the fingers close to the keys and roll the groups inward and upward, tossing off sharply on the last note. This gives a "sparkle" not obtainable with the usual finger legato.

Preparatory Exercise

March of the Gnomes

Allegretto

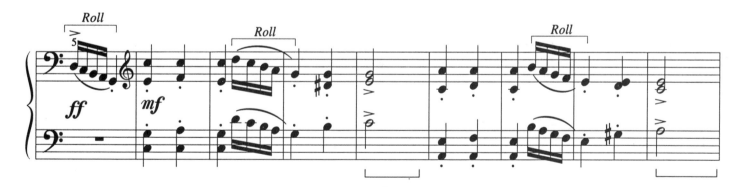

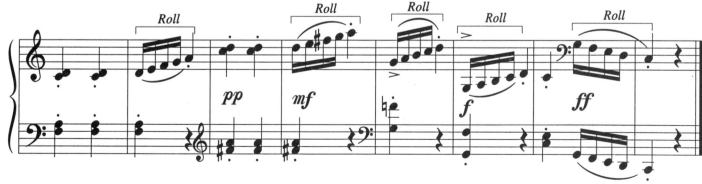

From old Vienna, the Austrian city of melody, comes this wistful song, transcribed here for piano. Play it with sympathetic expression, following phrasing and expression marks closely and using the pedal exactly as indicated. A good singing tone is essential.

A Viennese Melody

Andante con moto

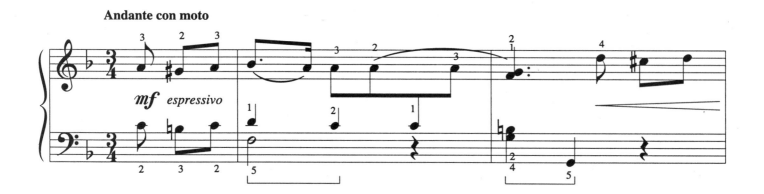

Jocularity

Scale Fingering Chart

SCALES BEGINNING ON WHITE KEYS

Right Hand
The Thumb falls on the FIRST and FOURTH notes of the scale.

Left-Hand
The Thumb falls on the FIRST and FIFTH notes of the scale.

FINGER GUIDE
THIRD FINGERS OF BOTH HANDS
ALWAYS PLAY TOGETHER.

There are two exceptions to the above rules-- the scales of B major and F major. They are fingered as follows:

B MAJOR ---Begin with FOURTH finger in the left hand.
F MAJOR---End with FOURTH finger in the right hand.

FINGER GUIDE
(for exceptional scales)
THUMBS OF BOTH HANDS
ALWAYS PLAY TOGETHER.

MINOR SCALES
The WHITE KEY MINOR Scales are fingered exactly the same as the WHITE KEY MAJOR Scales.

SCALES BEGINNING ON BLACK KEYS

MAJOR SCALES

Right Hand
Fourth finger on B♭ (or A#).

Left Hand
Fourth finger on the 4th note of the scale. Begin with THIRD finger.

There is one exception to the above rules~the major scale on G♭(or F#). For this scale use the rule of TWO'S and THREE'S, i.e., where TWO **BLACK** KEYS lie together, use the fingers 2 and 3. Where THREE **BLACK** KEYS lie together use the fingers 2, 3 and 4.

MINOR SCALES

B♭ MINOR ⎱ *TWO'S and THREE'S in*
E♭ MINOR ⎰ *BOTH hands.*

A♭ (or G#) MINOR-*Fingered same as MAJOR.*

Right Hand

D♭ (C#) MINOR ⎰ *FOURTH finger on the 2nd note of scale.*

Left Hand

G♭ (F#) MINOR ⎱ *TWO'S and THREE'S*

The Three Minor Forms

SHOWING THE EVOLUTION OF THE MINOR SCALE

C Major Scale

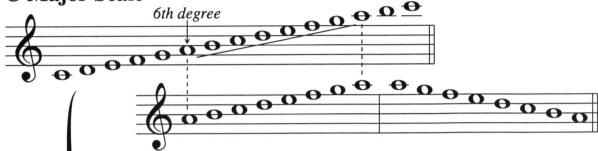

NATURAL MINOR FORM: This is the oldest form of the MINOR SCALE. Beginning on the 6th degree, it is ascended and descended on exactly the same notes contained in the RELATIVE MAJOR SCALE.

A MINOR

SCALE

RELATIVE

TO

C MAJOR

SCALE

6th and 7th raised. Descends same as the Natural form

MELODIC MINOR FORM: This form appeared at a later period. It was felt that in order to establish the "feel" of the tonality in A MINOR a leading tone (raised 7th) was necessary. However, the skip of a tone-and-a-half (from the 6th to the raised 7th) was unpleasant to ears not accustomed to such jumps. To obviate this, the 6th was also raised one half-step. Since a leading tone is not necessary in descending, the ME-LODIC MINOR scale descends on the same notes as those that make up the RELATIVE MAJOR Scale.

7th degree raised

HARMONIC MINOR FORM: This form is most frequently used in present day music. The 7th degree is raised one half-step both in ascending and descending.

GLOSSARY

of

Terms, Abbreviations and Signs used in
John Thompson's
SECOND GRADE BOOK

Abbreviation	TERMS	Signs	Abbreviation	TERMS	Signs
	Accent: Emphasize or stress.......	>∧	*legg..*	**Leggiero**: Light, easy, nimble.	
	Alla Breve: Two beats to the measure- one beat to each half note...................	¢		**Mezzo Forte**: Moderately loud. **Mezzo Piano**: Moderately soft.	*mf* *mp*
allarg.	**Allargando**: A slackening of the tempo..			**Moderato**: Moderately. **Molto**: Much.	
	Allegretto: Happy and moderately lively.			**Non Troppo**: Not to much. **Pause**: To hold or prolong beyond	⌢
	Allegro: Quick and cheerful. **Andante**: Moderately slow.			the allotated time......... **Piano**: Softly.	*p*
	Andantino: A little faster than Andante.			**Pianissimo**: Very softly........... **Poco**: Little.	*pp*
	Animato: Animated. **A Tempo**: Resume original speed.			**Poco a Poco**: Little by little. **Presto**: Quick, nimble, rapid.	
	Cadence: The end of a musical sentence.			**Reverie**: A dreamy composition.	
	Chromatic: Proceeding by half- steps.		*rit.*	**Ritardando**: A gradual slowing of the time.	
	Con Anima: With animation. **Con Brio**: With brilliance.			**Romanza**: Romance. **Scherzindo**: Playfully, gaily.	
cresc.	**Con Moto**: With motion. **Crescendo**: A gradual increasing	<	*scherz.*	**Scherzino**: A short composition in playful or whimsical style.	
	in tone. Shown also with the sign.			**Semplice**: Simply. **Sempre**: Always.	
D.C. al Fine	**Da Capo Al Fine**: Return to the beginning of the piece and play to		*sfz*	**Sforzando**: Forcing: the sudden accenting of a note or chord....	
	the end of the measure marked Fine.		*ten.*	**Sostenuto**: Sustained. Indicated by a line over a note or chord...	
Dim.	**Diminuendo**: A gradual decreas- ing in tone. Shown also.............	>	*stacc.*	**Staccato**: Detached................. **Staccatissimo**: Very short and	
	Dolce: Sweetly.			detached...............................	
Dom.	**Dominant**: The 5th degree of the scale.	V	*Subdom.*	**Subdominant**: The 4th degree of the scale>	IV
	e: And **Espressivo**: With expression.			**Syncopation**: Caused when ac- cents fall upon weak beats, mean-	
	Forte: Loud: Strong. **Fortissimo**: Very loud: very	*f* *ff*		while suppressing the nat- ural accented beats.	
	strong..................................... **Giocoso**: Sportively.			**Tempo**: Time. **Tempo I**: Resume original Time.	I
	Grace Notes: Little notes added as ornaments to give a graceful			**Tonic**: The 1st degree, or key- note of the scale.	
	effect. They have no time value and should be played as quickly as			**Trill**: A bird-like effect produced by rapidly alternatingtwo adjoining	*tr*
	possible.............................. **Grazioso**: Gracefully: smoothly.			notes of the same value. **Triplets**: Three notes of equal value	
	Leger Lines: Added lines above or below the staff.			played in the time of two notes of the same value.	3
	Legato: Smooth and connected.			**Vivace**: Lively, vivacious, light, gay.	

TECHNICAL DRILLS

Additional exercises to be assigned at the option of the teacher during the study of this book. Each has a specific purpose.

Trill for 1-2 and 4-5

Trill for 3-2 and 3-4

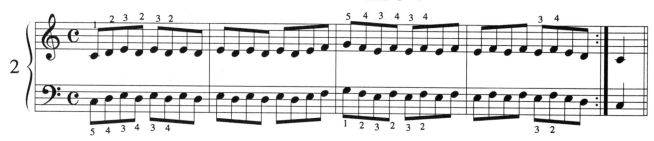

Combined Trill Figures

Passing the Thumb under the Second Finger
Follow the fingering exactly

Right Hand

Left Hand

Passing the Thumb under the Third Finger

Right Hand

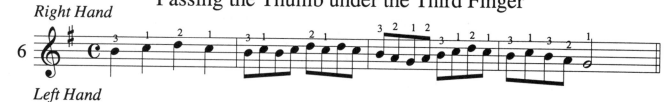

Left Hand

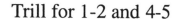

Passing the Thumb Under the Fourth Finger

The Chromatic Scale

Passing the Hand Over in Arpeggio Figures

Wrist Staccato (Sixths)

Certificate of Merit

This certifies that

_____

Has successfully completed
John Thompson's Second Grade Book

and is eligible for promotion to
John Thompson's Third Grade Book

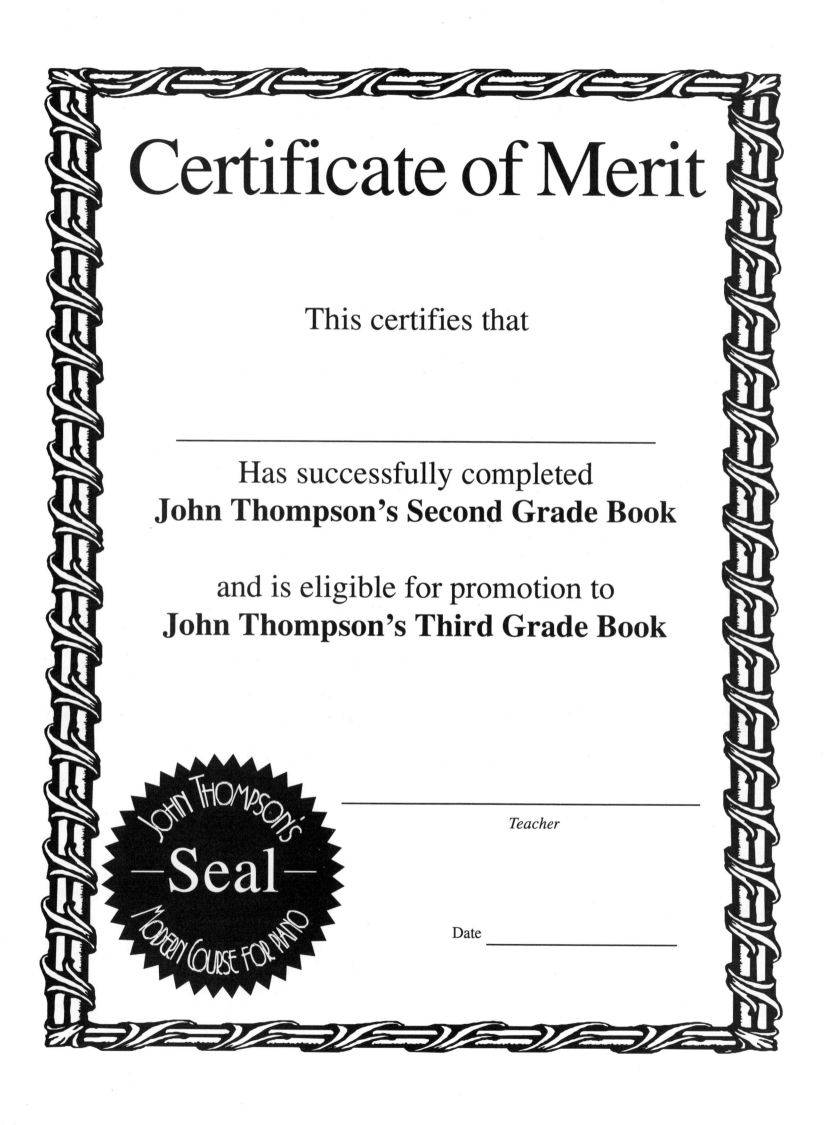

_____
Teacher

Date _____

THE PROGRESSIVE SUCCESSION
of
JOHN THOMPSON'S
MODERN COURSE FOR THE PIANO
"SOMETHING NEW EVERY LESSON"

PREPARATORY GRADE

Teaching Little Fingers to Play *A book for the earliest beginner combining ROTE and NOTE approach.*
Accompaniment Book : *Teaching Little Fingers to Play Ensemble*
With these accompaniments, teacher, parent, or advanced student may play each piece as a duet. The second piano part is invaluable for two-piano, four-hand playing in class or recital.

GRADE ONE

John Thompson's First Grade Book *A correct foundation for teaching the pupil to think and feel musically.*

Hanon Studies (*Specially edited by John Thompson*) *Pages 2-23 (in quarter-notes) to be used for supplementary work.*

Supplementary material for diversion
For Girls Who Play · Covered Wagon Suite
Let's Join the Army · Students Series —*Grade 1 Teaching Pieces*

GRADE TWO

John Thompson's Second Grade Book *Carries on the principles of the course "make haste slowly but learn thoroughly."*

Hanon Studies (*Specially edited by John Thompson*) *Pages 24-43 to be used supplementary.*
First Studies in Style
Supplementary material for diversion
The Pilgrim Suite · Students Series —*Grade 2 Teaching Pieces*

GRADE THREE

John Thompson's Third Grade Book *Progresses uninterruptedly and logically.*
Third Grade Velocity Studies (*Specially edited by John Thompson*)
Hanon Studies—Book Two (*Specially edited by John Thompson*)
Keyboard Attacks · World Known Melodies
Students Series —*Grade 3 Teaching Pieces*

FOR SALE BY ALL MUSIC DEALERS

Published by THE WILLIS MUSIC CO. Florence, Kentucky 41022-0548

JOHN THOMPSON

Talented American pianist-composer John Thompson was born in Pennsylvania. At an early age he appeared as a concert pianist in all of the principal cities of America and Europe, where his brilliant playing received the highest praise. After concluding his triumphant concert career he headed music departments at conservatories in Philadelphia, Indianapolis and Kansas City. During these tenures he developed certain definite and original ideas about teaching, and in a short time became famous for his sincere efforts to interest young pupils in pianism. All of his books teach, in the simplest language possible, interpretation and expression; one ideal, as it were: "to use in miniature the same attacks as those used by the concert artist."

COMPOSITIONS FOR PIANO SOLO

	Title	Grade	Key
4845	Air de Ballet. Op 43	3	E♭
5211	Castanets and Tambourines	3	Cm
4832	Columbine's Lament	2	Gm
5201	Faun	3	G
4831	Harlequin. Op. 42, No.1	3	C
5354	Les Clochettes	3	G
5271	Midnight Express	3	G
4774	Moths	3	G
5349	Petite Russian Rhapsodie	3	C
5670	Plantation Memories	3	C
4952	Polliwog	3	Dm
5200	Skater	3	D
4829	Sparks	2	Dm
4993	Wings	3	A
5245	Young American	3	G

ARRANGEMENTS OF FAMOUS MELODIES

	Title	Grade	Key
5277	Anitra's Dance (Grieg)	2.5	C
4911	Black Eyes (Russian Gypsy Folk-Song)	4	Dm
5204	Dream of Love (Liebesträume) (Liszt)	3.5	B♭
5231	Nocturne. Op. 23 (Schumann)	3	F
5229	On Wings of Song (Mendelssohn)	3	A♭
5279	Viennese Melody (Song Without Words)	3	G
5232	Waltz of the Flowers (from "The Nutcracker Suite," Tschaikowsky)	3	D

JOHN THOMPSON'S STUDENTS SERIES
PIANO SOLOS

GRADE I

5760	Barnyard Frolics	Blackford	G
5651	Cobbler, Cobbler	Rebe	G
5652	The Dutch Twins	Ward	C
5672	Forest Dawn	Thompson	C
5653	Hoe Cake Shuffle	Leslie	G
5784	In The Swing	Waldo	C
5648	Lullaby (Brahms)	Thompson	G
5650	March of the Spooks	Haines	Cm
5647	Marche Slave (Tschaikowsky)	Thompson	Am
5656	Moccasin Dance	Long	Am
5745	On the Levee	Waldo	C
5655	Procession of the Seven Dwarfs	Long	G
5657	Swaying Silver Birches	Leslie	C
5790	Twilight Lullaby	Haines	C

GRADE II

6337	The Banjo Picker	Wright	A
5724	Busy Corners	Montandon	C
5668	The Brownies Carnival	Thompson	C
5664	Captain Kidd	Waldo	Gm
5721	The Cheer Leader	Rodgers	C

GRADE II

5723	The Dirigible	Thompson	G
5785	Dreamy-Time Song	Munn	G
5666	Drowsy Moon	Long	G
5663	Hiawatha's Lullaby	Ward	G
5669	On a Summer Sea	Ketterer	C
5726	Parade of the Penguins	Wade	Am
5719	Roguish Eyes	Haines	G
5665	The Swan on the Moonlit Lake	Rebe	G
5792	Swinging High and Low	Cobb	D
5747	Under Southern Skies	Martin	C
5709	Woods at Dawn	Kerr	F

GRADE III

5717	Balloons	Arlen	A♭
5674	By a Roadside Fire	Rodgers	F
5722	The Drum Major	Selby	G
5665	March of the Champions	Waldo	G
5671	Tango Carioca	Thompson	Gm
5786	Three Blind Mice (Variations on the Theme)	Thompson	G-Gm-B♭
5720	The Wounded Gladiator	Long	Cm

PIANO FOUR HANDS

5690	Down the Shady Path	Jenkins
5687	Flame Vine	Bilbro
5688	In the Morning Early	Jenkins
5791	Spirit of the U.S.A.	Cobb
5689	The Strolling Players	Jenkins
5718	Tulip Time	Broaddus

Published by THE WILLIS MUSIC CO. Florence, Kentucky 41022-0548